I Am a
TIGER

Level 1

Written by Lori C. Froeb

Silver Dolphin

PRE-LEVEL 1: ASPIRING READERS

 LEVEL 1: EARLY READERS

- Basic factual texts with familiar themes and content
- Concepts in text are reinforced by photos
- Includes glossary to reinforce reading comprehension
- Phonic regularity
- Simple sentence structure and repeated sentence patterns
- Easy vocabulary familiar to kindergarteners and first graders

 LEVEL 2: DEVELOPING READERS

 LEVEL 3: ENGAGED READERS

 LEVEL 4: FLUENT READERS

Silver Dolphin Books
An imprint of Printers Row Publishing Group
A division of Readerlink Distribution Services, LLC
10350 Barnes Canyon Road, Suite 100, San Diego, CA 92121
www.silverdolphinbooks.com

ISBN: 978-1-68412-802-0
Manufactured, printed, and assembled in Shenzhen, China.
First printing, March 2019. RRD/03/19
23 22 21 20 19 1 2 3 4 5

Raaar! I am a tiger cub.

I am small now.

One day I will be a big cat.

Tigers are the biggest cats on earth!

There are six kinds of tigers alive today.

All tigers live in Asia.

Asia is a large **continent**.

Bengal tiger

Malayan tiger

Can you tell us apart?

ASIA

South
China tiger

Siberian tiger

Indochinese
tiger

Sumatran tiger

I am a Siberian tiger.
My family lives in a country called Russia.
Siberia is part of Russia.

We live in the forest.
It can get very cold in winter!

RUSSIA

I live here!

The world has many big cats.

cheetah

jaguar

tiger

lion

leopard

Siberian tigers are the biggest cats of all.

I will be six hundred pounds one day.

My body will be ten feet long from head to tail!

All tigers have striped coats.
Our skin is striped, too.
The stripes are **camouflage**.

They help us blend in with the grass and trees.

We hide from our **prey**. We sneak closer until it is time to pounce.

Tigers are carnivores.
That means we eat meat.

We eat a lot at once.
We do not always eat
every day.

I am too young to hunt.
My mom hunts for our food.
My sister and I watch her.
We will learn to hunt from her.

Most of the time mom hunts for wild boar.

They are pigs with long hair.

She also hunts for elk and even bears.

Sometimes large prey is hard to find.

Then mom brings us rabbits or fish!

We cannot wait to hunt on our own.

Tigers are expert hunters.
Our bodies are made for it!

legs

Our back legs are strong.
We can leap thirty feet!

ears

We can **swivel** our ears to hear prey.

eyes

We can see very well in day or night.

teeth

Our teeth can be three inches long. They grip and tear prey.

feet

Our padded feet are very quiet. This makes it easy to surprise prey.

Adult tigers do not live in groups. Adult tigers live and hunt alone. I will stay with my mother until I am two.

Then I will find a **territory** of my own.

A territory is where a tiger lives and hunts.

Tigers mark their territory.

We scratch trees with our nails.

Other tigers see the scratches.

The scratches mean the
area belongs to another tiger.

Our nails can be four inches long!

They are tucked in when not being used.

They stay very sharp.

We also use urine (pee) to mark things.

Mom is not smiling here! She is sniffing the scent left by another tiger.

She opens her mouth to get a better sniff.

She learns about the other tiger.

She can tell if it is male or female and how old it is.

I try to sniff, too!

Most cats do not like the water.
Tigers are not like most cats.
We like the water!

We play in the water and take baths.

Tigers are also great swimmers.

Some have swum miles to cross rivers.

We also use sound to talk to each other.

A tiger's roar can be heard two miles away!

We can also growl and hiss.
We cannot purr like house
cats.

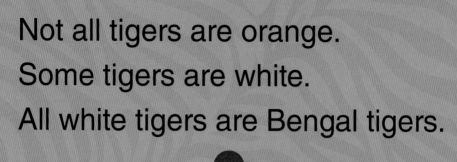

Not all tigers are orange.

Some tigers are white.

All white tigers are Bengal tigers.

White tigers have blue eyes.
About one white tiger is born out
of ten thousand cubs.

There are about two hundred
white tigers on Earth.

There used to be many tigers in the wild.

Now there are less than four thousand left.

Our **habitats** are shrinking.

Humans hunt us.

We are **endangered**.
This means we may one day disappear.

If humans protect us, we will survive.

We will rule the jungle once again!

Glossary

camouflage: an animal's coloring that helps it hide and blend in

continent: one of seven large pieces of land on earth

endangered: almost none left in the world

habitat: the place where an animal lives

prey: an animal that is hunted by other animals for food

swivel: to move in different directions

territory: the area where an animal lives and hunts